98

Also by Deborah Chandra

Balloons and Other Poems
with pictures by Leslie Bowman

Rich Lizard and Other Poems

Rich Lizard

and Other Poems

Deborah Chandra

Pictures by Leslie Bowman

Farrar Straus Giroux
New York

For Kenneth and for Neva Hamlin
—from the wilds of Linwood Street
D.C.

For Margaret, for being there
L.B.

Contents

Rich Lizard and Other Poems

Grandpa's Shoes

Lying by the back door,
Grandpa's shoes
speak in a husky
whisper:
      "Step inside," they say.
      "We're big and bruised
        and scuffed, but
        down past the tough
        we've worn ourselves soft.

      "We've been somewhere."

Bubble

I made my lips grow
close and round,
and blew
into a plastic wand.
Then I saw it,
clear and thin—
my breath
wrapped in a
quivering skin
of soap that held
the blue of sky,
the sudden flash
of fireflies.
It made a trembling
shadow there,
slid whispering
through empty air,
to dip and soar
while full of glow,
I was surprised,
I didn't know
my own breath
could be a thing
so marble-round,
and glistening.

The Wild Wood

Down at the curb where cars go by,
Between leaves where two hedges meet,
I can disappear through an opening
Like a door off a noisy street.

There, in the warm hollow darkness
Inside the hedges' green,
I enter a wild twilight wood,
Where sounds come as faint and strange

As the far-off roar of a waterfall
Where black bears prowl and eat,
And I hide behind its silvery spray—
In there, where two hedges meet.

Cricket

A metal bug
with rusty tongue,
and throat stuck shut.

The song he makes
comes chiseled off,
small scrapes,
tin flakes.

His voice opens,
closes,
on a hinge.
A metal self
is all he's got.
He stops.

Winds a spring,
kicks stiff bolts,
then on he sings
with raspy bits of
rusted things.

Porch Light

At night
the porch light
catches moths
and holds them,
trapped
and
flapping,
in a tight
yellow fist.
Only when I
turn the switch
will it loosen
its hot
grip.

Rich Lizard

The rich lizard
shed his skin
of silver coins,
dropping them
in the dry grass.
Strange-wild thoughts
shook him,
warming his blood
to grander things,
and he tore himself
loose—
ran off,
leaving behind
his wealth of cold coins.

What the Ant Says

Through the greenest
depth of grasses,
there Old Brown Snail
slowly passes,
hiding in shadows
from the moon.

He keeps his shell
a darkened room.
Inside his room—
a winding stair.
It is damp and gloomy there!

Snail won't tell,
so no one knows
where his winding stairway goes.
But I am not afraid
to peek
into his room
when he's asleep,
and climb the narrow steps
. . . and yet,
the way is steep
and dark and wet,
and there echoes round and round
a cold and hollow
sound!

Green Gloves

Spring
took the
icy
hands of Winter
in her own,
and stuck them
in green gloves.

Poppies

They rustle their gypsy skirts,
Spreading them cleverly;
Their red breath blooms
Into little wild whisperings.
With bold black eyes they smile

At my lips, my hands, my hair,
While something is hidden—
Amid the bright rustlings,
Amid the little warm whisperings
Of wild things.

Clouds

Herded
and
hurried
by the wind,
surrounded
by the horizon,
a billowing
bunch of sheep
leap—
frightened
and trembling
in their damp
wool coats.

Kite

I skitter over rooftops
On a river of wind
That rattles my bones,
Reshapes my skin,
Taking me over the tallest trees,
I'm slide-fall-running
With the leaves,
And rush along
The wind to find:
Soft dust floating from Africa,
Hissing whispers of loose air,
Broken stars, mists,
Cloud fluff,
Sounds that only dogs can hear,
Blue chimney smoke and shadow-swarm,
The moon's white eye,
The smell of storms.

Now the wind whips me round,
Seizes my skin,
Tumbles me down
To earth,
Where I lie dazed—for I
Have felt and touched and tasted sky.

Statue in the Park

Across the grass
and down a walk,
I met a lady
made of rock.
I stretched up on my toes
to see
into her face.
She looked at me,
but didn't smile
or speak,
or move.
I saw her skin
was hard and smooth,
and knew that she would
never cry,
standing strong,
head up high.
—But she couldn't
sing
the way I could.
I sang to her,
and so we stood,
a little while, there,
side by side,
the lady made of rock,
and I.

The Argument

Her words rose, swarming round,
Ugly, stinging shapes of sound,
Circling the foe.

His words bristled, black with warning,
Arched and stiff, they met the swarming,
Hissing low.

They sprang and clawed and stung in space,
But shaped as words, they left no trace
Of fur or fang about the place.

Outside Overnight

I carried out the sleeping bags,
Lee carried out her long flashlight;
We left the house behind and went
Into the chilly back-yard night.

The flashlight cut a yellow beam,
Dark moths fluttered out, then in;
The grass around the bags grew wet,
We pulled the zippers to our chins.

When Lee turned her flashlight off,
We felt the darkness overhead
Slide silently between the trees
And softly wrap around our beds.

"Look," she whispered — all about
Small stars shivered in the cold
And stirred as if to snuggle down
Into the night sky's velvet folds.

The dark unrolled and deeply spread
Its thick black edges, zippered tight,
So Lee and I could fall asleep,
Tucked inside the back-yard night.

Cotton Candy

Swirling
like a sweet
tornado,
it spins itself
stiff.
A storm
caught on a paper cone.
I hold it up,
the air grows
thick and
sticky
with the smell of it.
A pink wind
made of sugar
and smoke,
cotton,
earth crust,
delicious dust!

Sandman

At the beach I dug wet sand
That molded easy in my hands.

I packed it and a sandman grew,
I searched along the shore for two

Gray shells for eyes, a stone for nose.
Then I gave him seaweed clothes.

All day long he stayed by me
And watched me play. He didn't leave.

Even when the sun got hot,
He stayed and made a shady spot.

But evening came, the sea swirled round
His feet, and made a sucking sound.

It washed away one leg; white foam
Sprayed higher. He was all alone.

I didn't want to see him go.
I touched him. I told him so.

But as the waves rolled out, then in,
He crumbled—and I stayed by him.

Moon Baby

From the window
looking up,
baby lifts
his drinking cup;
claps his hands,
bangs his spoon,
and laughs—
reaching for the moon.
He watches how
a strange white light
dribbles down
into the night,
but doesn't see
his shadow crawl
across the table
to the wall.
It slowly rises,
stretches, stands,
with longer body,
thicker hands,
as if from baby's
small round limbs
comes someone
tightly curled in him.

My Tooth

Beneath
my pillow,
buried deep
like treasure,
from the dark it speaks
of ivory crumbled
with sharp stone,
of crystal ground
with tooth and bone,
of marble crushed
with pearl: when mixed
and sifted down
will shine, and with
one quick pinch
of powdered tusk,
makes magic —
makes the fairies' dust.

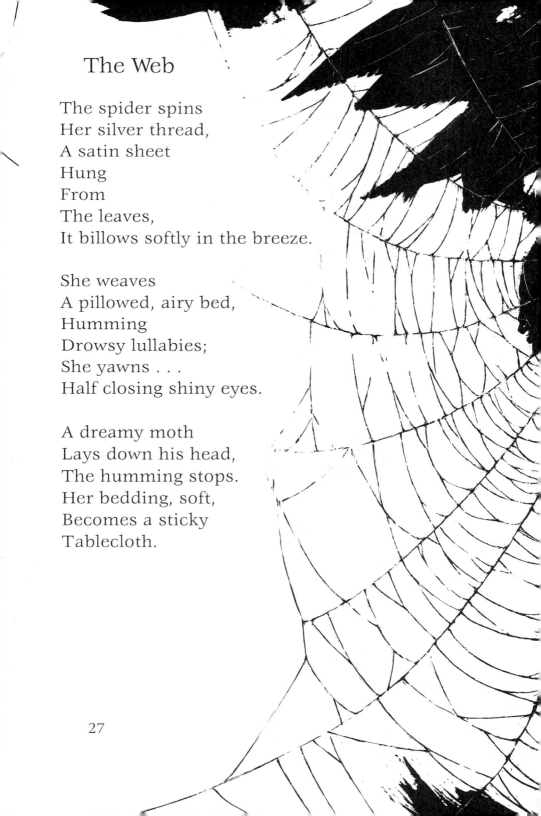

The Web

The spider spins
Her silver thread,
A satin sheet
Hung
From
The leaves,
It billows softly in the breeze.

She weaves
A pillowed, airy bed,
Humming
Drowsy lullabies;
She yawns . . .
Half closing shiny eyes.

A dreamy moth
Lays down his head,
The humming stops.
Her bedding, soft,
Becomes a sticky
Tablecloth.

Fox

Down from the mountains
Into camp,
The air was cold,
Earth lay damp,
Came a silver fox.
Slyly, she'd say:
   "They all will sleep till the stars slip away."

On delicate feet
She drifted like smoke,
From trees
To cot,
From cot
To coals.
The fire drowsed.
Smiling, she'd say:
   "All will sleep till the stars slip away."

Ears stood pricked,
Her warm breath curled,
She tasted air,
Yet the wildness in her
Never sensed,
With quick eyes
Or cautious paws,
How I watched her:
   Till she slipped away with the stars.

29

The River Speaks

I am old with flowing
Past bush and boulder
Of dry land.
Tumbling down,
Stumbling on,
Reaching out
With pale wet hands
To roots, rocks,
And silent leaves,
Knocking on
The earth's stone door,
Calling out to
Reeds and twigs—

    They watch me pass,
    Nothing more.

Who will hear
My wandering voice,
Take my watery hands in theirs,
Hold me close
And still my flowing;
Where am I going?
Where?

The Storm's Gold

Deep inside the clouds' gray hills
Of storm-dark rock and stone,
The miners dig. They're searching for
The lightning's vein of gold.

When the lightning flashes,
They mark it with a spike,
Then come the wondrous thunderings
Of miners' dynamite.

Late August

Late August splits its skin,
It is so ripe;
Full of sunburned days,
Plum-colored nights.
Swaying with its weight,
The branches bend
When warm air rustles
Through the trees and sends
The branches slowly bobbing
Up and down.
Late August, round with
Summertime,
Holds on.

Day's End

Where
does
the day
go —
when it
crumples
like old
newspaper,
to rattle
and flit
in the
night
wind?